UNPLUG WITH SCIENCE BUDDIES

FUN WITH NATURE PROJECTS

Bubble Wands,
Sunset in a Glass,
and More

Megan Borgert-Spaniol

Lerner Publications ◆ Minneapolis

Lerner Publications Company
A division of Lerner Publishing Group, Inc.
241 First Avenue North
Minneapolis, MN 55401 USA
For reading levels and more information, look up this title at www.lernerbooks.com.

Main body text set in Zemestro Std Book 12/16
Typeface provided by Monotype Imaging Inc.

Photo Acknowledgements
The images in this book are used with the permission of: Design elements and doodles © frozenbunn/Shutterstock, © mhatzapa/Shutterstock, © Mighty Media, Inc., © primiaou/Shutterstock, © Sashatigar/Shutterstock, © STILLFX/Shutterstock, © Sudowoodo/Shutterstock, © Tiwat K/Shutterstock, © Tom and Kwikki/Shutterstock; © roberthyrons/iStockphoto, p. 4 (leaves); © knape/iStockphoto, p. 5; © baona/iStockphoto, p. 6; © Mighty Media, Inc., pp. 7 (clay, leaves, jar, flashlight, yarn, card stock), 8–29 (project photos); © CasarsaGuru/iStockphoto, p. 30

Front and back covers: © Mighty Media, Inc.

Library of Congress Cataloging-in-Publication Data

Names: Borgert-Spaniol, Megan, 1989– author.
Title: Fun with nature projects : bubble wands, sunset in a glass, and more / Megan Borgert-Spaniol.
Description: Minneapolis : Lerner Publications, [2020] | Series: Unplug with science buddies | Includes bibliographical references and index. | Audience: Age 7–11. | Audience: Grade 4 to 6.
Identifiers: LCCN 2018058303 (print) | LCCN 2019000019 (ebook) | ISBN 9781541562448 (eb pdf) | ISBN 9781541554962 (lb : alk. paper) | ISBN 9781541574892 (pb : alk. paper)
Subjects: LCSH: Natural history—Experiments—Juvenile literature.
Classification: LCC QH55 (ebook) | LCC QH55 .B67 2020 (print) | DDC 508.072/3—dc23

LC record available at https://lccn.loc.gov/2018058303

Manufactured in the United States of America

Contents

Nature Unplugged

Have you ever wondered why bubbles pop? How thermometers measure temperature? Where the brilliant colors of fall leaves and fireworks come from?

You can learn a lot about science by observing the natural world. And you don't need fancy lab equipment, computer software, or other technology to do it! You can do experiments in nature or inspired by nature with some household items and a bit of curiosity.

And the fun doesn't need to end once you've made your creation. Think of ways to experiment with your project. What can you discover? Let's unplug and start making!

Before You Get Started

SUPPLY CHECK

Many of the projects in this book use common household items and craft supplies. These can include drinking straws, dish soap, and table salt. Other materials can be found at the grocery store, hardware store, or office supply store.

SAFETY FIRST

The projects in this book may use hot objects or messy ingredients. Several projects require a safe and open outdoor space to work in. Ask an adult for permission before starting a project, and request help when needed.

CLEANING UP

When you've completed a project, remember to clean up! Put supplies back where you found them, throw away garbage, wipe up spills, and wash dirty dishes. If you want to keep your creation, be sure to store it in a safe place!

MAKE A RAINBOW

Rainbows appear when sunlight shines through water droplets in the atmosphere. Create your own mini rainbow using water, paper, and sunlight!

MATERIALS

- ☆ shallow glass baking pan
- ☆ water
- ☆ outdoor chair or table
- ☆ white, blue, and red sheets of paper
- ☆ sunlight

SCIENCE TAKEAWAY

Sunlight is made up of all the colors of the visible light spectrum. When sunlight passes through water, all the colors bend at slightly different angles. This is why we see rainbows after rain. Rainbows appear differently on blue and red paper because these paper types do not reflect all colors of visible light.

1 Fill the pan about halfway with water.

2 Place the pan on a chair or table outside in the sun. One end of the pan should stick out past the edge of the surface. Make sure it doesn't stick out so far that it falls off.

3 Place the white paper on the ground where the sun is shining through the pan.

4 Change the angle of the paper until a small rainbow forms. Adjust the angle of the paper until you create the largest rainbow possible. Note which colors you see.

5 Place the blue paper on top of the white paper. How does the rainbow change when you switch between the blue and the white?

6 Remove the blue paper and place the red paper on top of the white paper. How does the rainbow change when you switch between the red and the white?

SUNSET IN A JAR

As the sun sets, the color of the sky changes from blue to orange to red. You can create your own sunset using a flashlight and milk!

MATERIALS

- ☆ tall jar or glass that can hold at least 16 ounces (0.5 L)
- ☆ water
- ☆ non-LED flashlight
- ☆ whole milk
- ☆ teaspoon

SCIENCE TAKEAWAY

The particles in Earth's atmosphere scatter blue light more than other colors of light. The scattered blue light makes the sky appear blue. At sunrise and sunset, sunlight travels farther through the atmosphere. By the time that light reaches us, most of the blue light has scattered away, making the sky appear red and orange. In your jar, the fat droplets in the milk act like the particles in Earth's atmosphere. The farther the light travels through the jar, the more blue light is scattered away.

1 Fill the jar with water.

2 Shine the flashlight through the side of the jar. What color is the water?

3 Stir about 1 teaspoon of milk into the water. What color is the solution?

4 Shine the flashlight through the side of the jar. Did the color of the solution change?

5 Hold the flashlight above the jar so it shines down through the solution. Does the color of the solution change from the top of the jar to the bottom?

CRANBERRY VOLCANO

Most liquids are either an acid or a base. Try testing acidic and basic liquids using cranberry juice!

MATERIALS

- ☆ 2 lemons
- ☆ knife
- ☆ juicer
- ☆ small bowl
- ☆ 4 glasses
- ☆ marker
- ☆ tape
- ☆ measuring cups and spoons
- ☆ water
- ☆ 3 cups pure, 100 percent cranberry juice
- ☆ large baking pan
- ☆ baking soda

SCIENCE TAKEAWAY

Cranberry juice has pigments that become lighter when reacting with an acid and darker when reacting with a base. The reaction of baking soda (a base) with cranberry juice (slightly acidic) releases a gas. This gas creates foamy bubbles. Adding lemon juice (an acid) neutralizes the liquid, changing its color back to normal.

1 Have an adult cut the lemon in half. Use a juicer to squeeze the juice out of the lemons. Pour the lemon juice into a small bowl. Set the bowl aside.

2 Use the marker and tape to label one of the glasses "water." Label the other three glasses with numbers 1, 2, and 3.

3 Pour 1 cup of water into the water glass. Set the glass aside.

4 Pour 1 cup of cranberry juice into each of the other three glasses.

Cranberry Volcano continued on next page

5 Place the three glasses of juice side by side in the baking pan.

6 Stir 2 tablespoons of lemon juice into glass 1. Compare the color of the juice in glass 1 to the color of the juice in glass 2.

7 Add 1 tablespoon of baking soda to glass 3. What happens? Observe the reaction until it stops foaming.

8 Look at the juice in glass 3. Compare it to the juice in glass 2. What is different between the two?

9 Now compare the color and volume of all three glasses. Which glass is the most different from the others?

10 Add 2 tablespoons of lemon juice to glass 3. What happens? Observe the reaction until it stops foaming. Did anything change about glass 3 after you added the lemon juice?

11 Stir 2 tablespoons of baking soda into the water glass. Does anything happen?

BOTTLE THERMOMETER

Liquid-filled thermometers have been used to measure temperature for centuries. Find out how these simple instruments work by making your own thermometer out of a bottle and a straw!

MATERIALS

- ☆ fine-tipped permanent marker
- ☆ clear plastic drinking straw
- ☆ ruler
- ☆ modeling clay
- ☆ small narrow-necked plastic bottle with lid (empty food coloring bottles work well)
- ☆ rubbing alcohol
- ☆ food coloring
- ☆ medicine dropper
- ☆ paper towel
- ☆ small bowl
- ☆ water
- ☆ ice cubes

SCIENCE TAKEAWAY

As things heat up or cool down, the amount of space they take up changes. Liquid-filled thermometers use this change to measure temperature. As the temperature increases, the liquid expands up through the thermometer. As the temperature decreases, the liquid shrinks back down.

1 Use permanent marker to draw short lines from one end of the straw to the other. The lines should be spaced 0.2 inches (0.5 cm) apart.

2 Form a ball of modeling clay about 1 inch (2.3 cm) across. Press the ball flat. Make sure the clay shape is bigger than the bottle's opening.

3 Punch a hole in the middle of the clay shape with the straw. The hole should be just big enough to allow the straw through. Remove any clay from inside the straw.

4 Fill the bottle about half full with rubbing alcohol. Add a couple of drops of food coloring. Put the lid on the bottle and shake it to mix the liquids.

5 Dip the medicine dropper into the bottle. Fill it with colored rubbing alcohol. Carefully set the medicine dropper aside on a paper towel. Pour a little more rubbing alcohol into the bottle to fill it halfway again.

Bottle Thermometer continued on next page

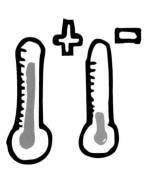

6 Place the clay over the bottle's neck so the straw hangs down into the bottle. Adjust the straw so the bottom end is in the liquid but not touching the bottom of the bottle. Most of the straw should be sticking out of the top of the bottle.

7 Press the modeling clay around the straw and the top of the bottle to form an airtight seal.

8 Drip the liquid in the medicine dropper, one drop at a time, into the top of the straw. The liquid should build up in the straw and stay there. If it runs into the bottle, check that the clay is forming an airtight seal around the straw and the neck of the bottle. Make sure the bottom end is in the liquid. Then try again.

9 Drop the liquid into the straw until the liquid reaches about halfway up the visible part of the straw. If needed, add more rubbing alcohol to the straw.

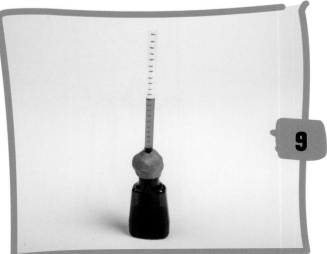

10 Observe the level of the liquid in the straw. This level indicates room temperature. Using the permanent marker, draw a small dot at the top of the liquid.

11 Fill the small bowl with medium-hot tap water. Place the bottle thermometer in the water. Wait for it to adjust to the new temperature. How does the level of the liquid change?

12 Replace the water in the bowl with cold tap water. Add a few ice cubes to the water. Let the bowl sit for a few minutes. Then place the bottle thermometer in the water. Wait for it to adjust to the new temperature. How does the level of the liquid change?

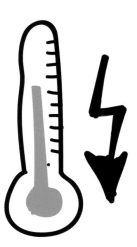

SUNDIAL TIME

The sundial is the oldest known instrument for telling time. It has a thin rod that casts a shadow onto a platform. As Earth spins, the rod's shadow moves, showing the passage of time!

MATERIALS

- ☆ pencil
- ☆ paper plate
- ☆ clock
- ☆ marker
- ☆ ruler
- ☆ plastic straw
- ☆ tape
- ☆ sunny outdoor space with no shadows
- ☆ rock or other weight

SCIENCE TAKEAWAY

As Earth spins, the sun's position relative to Earth changes. As a result, sunlight hits the straw of your sundial at different angles throughout the day. Earth spins 15 degrees every hour. Because of this, the shadow of your sundial's straw should also move about 15 degrees clockwise every hour.

1 Turn the paper plate upside down. Use a pencil to poke a hole through the center of the plate.

2 Check the time and round up to the nearest hour. Write this hour at the edge of the plate. For example, if the clock says 8:45 a.m., write "9" on the plate. Use the ruler to draw a straight line from the number you wrote to the hole in the center of the plate.

3 Push the straw through the hole in the plate. Tip the straw toward the line you drew. Tape the straw in place.

4 Wait until the clock reads the hour you wrote on the plate. Then, take the plate outside.

5 Put the plate on the ground in a sunny open space. Rotate the plate so the shadow of the straw lines up with the line on the plate. Place a rock or other weight on the plate to hold it in place.

6 After an hour, return to your sundial and observe the position of the shadow. So, if you started at 9:00 a.m., return to your sundial at 10:00 a.m. Write "10" on the edge of the plate where the shadow falls.

7 Check your sundial several more times. Wait an hour between each time. Each time you check it, write the hour on the plate where the shadow falls. Observe the sundial. What does it remind you of?

FLAMING FIREWORKS

Have you ever wondered how fireworks explode in so many different colors? These colors come from metals that burn when a firework goes off. Safely create your own small fireworks at home!

MATERIALS

- ☆ tablespoon
- ☆ table salt
- ☆ 2 small plastic bags
- ☆ 6 bamboo skewers
- ☆ white glue
- ☆ pure copper sulfate in the form of powder or small crystals (available at pet stores or home improvement stores)
- ☆ disposable gloves
- ☆ safety goggles
- ☆ small candle
- ☆ matches
- ☆ bucket of water
- ☆ open area outdoors

SCIENCE TAKEAWAY

The colors of fireworks come from the burning of different metals. You should see different colors when you burn table salt, also called sodium chloride, and copper sulfate. When the metal sodium is burned, it makes a yellow-orange light. Burning the metal copper makes a blue-green light.

1 Put about 1 tablespoon of salt in a small plastic bag.

2 Coat about 1 inch (2.5 cm) of the end of a skewer with glue.

3 Dip the glue-coated end of the skewer into the salt in the bag. Twist the skewer to coat the end with salt.

4 Set the skewer aside. Repeat steps 2 and 3 to make two more salt-tipped skewers.

5 Have an adult repeat steps 1 through 4, but with copper sulfate instead of salt. Anyone handling copper sulfate should wear disposable gloves and safety goggles.

6 Let the glue on all six skewers dry.

7 When it starts getting dark outside, take the candle, matches, skewers, and bucket of water to an open area.

8 Set the candle on the ground. Have an adult light it. Stand upwind of the flame so the breeze carries any smoke away from you.

9 Hold a salt-coated end of a skewer in the flame. Do not breathe the fumes or smoke from the burning skewer. What color does the salt burn? If the skewer catches fire, drop it into the bucket of water.

10 Repeat step 9 but with a copper sulfate-coated skewer. What color does the copper sulfate burn?

23

GREAT BIG BUBBLES

Bubbles need soap and water to form and hold their shape. Discover how these substances work together when you make your own bubble solution and giant bubble wand!

MATERIALS

- ☆ 2 wooden dowels at least 0.5 inches (1.3 cm) wide
- ☆ 2 screw eyes
- ☆ yarn
- ☆ measuring tape
- ☆ scissors
- ☆ washer
- ☆ measuring cups and spoons
- ☆ water
- ☆ liquid dish soap
- ☆ glycerin
- ☆ baking powder
- ☆ large bucket
- ☆ open area outdoors

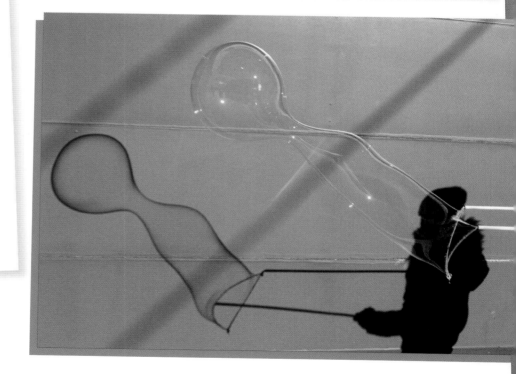

SCIENCE TAKEAWAY

A bubble is a layer of water between two layers of soap. When the water evaporates, the bubble pops. Glycerin thickens the layers of soap, preventing the water from evaporating. Larger bubbles have more weight to support. They also have more surface area across which evaporation can occur. So, larger bubbles pop more easily.

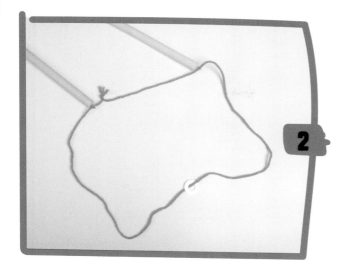

1 Have an adult help you attach a screw eye to one end of each dowel.

2 Cut a piece of yarn that is 3 feet (1 m) long. Thread the yarn through the washer. Then thread it through both screw eyes. Tie the ends of the yarn together to form a large loop. This is your bubble wand.

3 Put 8 cups of water, ½ cup of liquid dish soap, 1 tablespoon of glycerin, and 1 tablespoon of baking powder in a bucket. This is your bubble solution.

4 Set the bucket outside in a large open area. Pull the measuring tape out at least 10 feet (3 m). Place the measuring tape on the ground extending from the bucket in the direction the wind is blowing.

5 Hold the ends of the dowels without the screw eyes. Move the two screw eyes together so they touch. Lower them and the yarn into the bubble solution.

6 Lift the wand from the bubble solution and move the ends of the dowels apart to open the yarn loop. Hold the open loop away from your body in the same direction as the measuring tape. How long is the largest bubble you can create?

7 Replace the yarn with a piece that is 6 feet (1.8 m) long. Then repeat steps 5 and 6 with the larger bubble wand. How long is the largest bubble you can create?

FALL COLOR CHEMISTRY

Tree leaves get their colors from pigments. The green pigment, chlorophyll, breaks down in fall. That's when yellow, orange, and red pigments become visible. Discover the pigments in fall leaves with this paper chromatography project!

MATERIALS

- ☆ fall leaves
- ☆ scissors
- ☆ 3 tall drinking glasses
- ☆ tablespoon
- ☆ rubbing alcohol
- ☆ wooden spoon
- ☆ shallow baking pan
- ☆ hot tap water
- ☆ fork
- ☆ 3 very small containers
- ☆ toothpicks
- ☆ extra-thick paper towels
- ☆ ruler
- ☆ pencils
- ☆ clothespins

SCIENCE TAKEAWAY

A leaf can have several different pigments even if it looks like just one color. These pigments can be revealed in a process called paper chromatography. In this process, you separate pigments by having them move up the paper at different speeds.

1 Collect leaves at different stages of color change during fall. Try to get them from the same tree. Separate your leaves into green, yellow, and red piles. You will need about ten leaves in each color group.

2 Cut the leaves in each color group into small pieces.

3 Put the leaf pieces for each color group in a different glass.

Fall Color Chemistry continued on next page

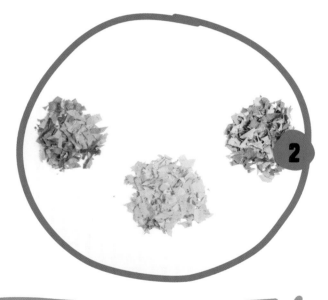

4 Add 1 tablespoon of rubbing alcohol to each glass. Use a wooden spoon to crush the leaves in each glass into the rubbing alcohol for about five minutes. This creates a dark solution in each glass.

5 Set the glasses in the baking pan. Fill the pan halfway with hot tap water. Leave the glasses sitting in the hot water for 30 minutes.

6 Use a fork to remove the leaf pieces from the glasses. Throw away the leaf pieces.

7 Pour each solution into its own very small container. Put the containers in a dark place indoors. Wait one hour.

8 Use a toothpick to stir one of the solutions. If it appears thicker, it is ready. If not, leave the solutions in the dark place another hour. When the solutions are ready, stir each with a different toothpick.

9 Cut three strips off a paper towel. Each strip should be 1 inch (2.5 cm) wide and longer than the glasses are tall.

10 Use a pencil to draw a line 1 inch (2.5 cm) from one end of each strip.

11 Use the toothpicks to paint the pencil line on each strip with one of the solutions. Let the strips dry.

12 Rinse out the drinking glasses. Pour a little rubbing alcohol into each glass so the liquid just covers the bottoms of the glasses.

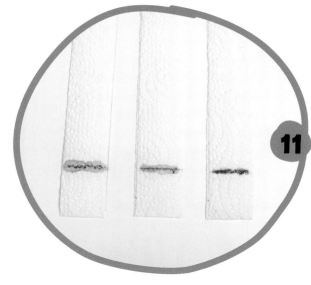

13 Place a paper towel strip in a glass. The bottom of the strip should just touch the rubbing alcohol. Lay a pencil across the top of the glass. Secure the top of the strip to the pencil with a clothespin. Make sure the strip is not touching the side of the glass.

14 Repeat step 13 with the other paper strips.

15 Observe the strips for about 20 minutes. What happens to the color painted onto the strips?

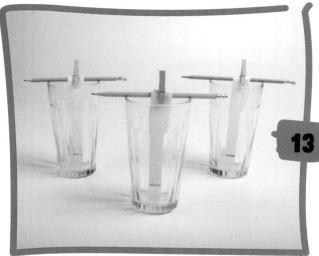

16 When the alcohol reaches the top of the paper strips, remove them from their glasses. Pour out any remaining rubbing alcohol. Hang the strips back in the empty glasses and let them dry. Can you see that leaves of the same color may contain different pigments?

Explore More!

What fun, nature-inspired projects did you complete? What did you learn as you experimented? Science is all around us, even when we aren't plugged into technology. And the more we experiment with science, the more we discover. So keep exploring new ways to experiment, discover, and have fun with nature!

FURTHER INFORMATION

For more information and projects, visit Science Buddies at https://www.sciencebuddies.org/.

Challoner, Jack. *Maker Lab Outdoors: 25 Super Cool Projects: Build, Invent, Create, Discover.* New York: DK Publishing, 2016.

Heinecke, Liz Lee. *Outdoor Science Lab for Kids: 52 Family-Friendly Experiments for the Yard, Garden, Playground, and Park.* Beverly, MA: Quarry Books, 2016.

Leigh, Anna. *30-Minute Outdoor Science Projects.* Minneapolis: Lerner Publications, 2019.

Glossary

acid: a substance with many hydrogen ions. Most acids have a sour taste.

atmosphere: the air that surrounds Earth

base: a substance with many hydroxide ions. Most bases have a bitter taste.

chromatography: a process in which a chemical mixture is separated into components

degree: a unit used to measure angles. There are 360 degrees in a complete circle.

evaporate: to change from liquid into gas

glycerin: a thick liquid that comes from plant and animal sources and attracts water

neutralize: to cause a chemical or solution to be neither an acid nor a base

pigment: a natural substance that gives color to animals or plants

solution: a mixture made up of one or more substances that have been dissolved in a liquid

visible light spectrum: the range of light wavelengths that can be seen by the human eye

Index